A Can of Pinto Beans

Robbie Gamble

LILY POETRY REVIEW BOOKS

Published by Lily Poetry Review Books
223 Winter Street
Whitman, MA 02382

https://lilypoetryreview.blog/

ISBN: 978-1-7375043-4-4

Published in the United States by Lily Poetry Review Books.
Library of Congress Control Number: 2021949292

Cover Design: Michael McInnis

TABLE OF CONTENTS

I believe the world is beautiful
and that poetry, like bread, is for everyone.
And that my veins don't end in me
but in the unanimous blood
of those who struggle for life,
love,
little things,
landscape and bread,
the poetry of everyone.

— Roque Dalton

AS THOMAS

As a nurse, I've known wounds:
gashes, ulcers, the delicate epithelium
weeping, seen and unseen.

Years ago, in a lull in the Salvadoran war,
I frequented a church
where scores
had been disappeared.

After Mass, an ancient woman tugged my sleeve.
said, you *extranjeros*,
are like Santo Tomás.

It was not enough to hear about
El Salvador:
you had to come
to see us,
touch our wounds.

How to stockpile
more gauze, more
salve, more
sustenance
for the journey?

To drag back up
after every darkness,
and see.

HUMAN REMAINS

—Arivaca, Arizona

Dusk, and she was driving
south on Rte. 286
to visit with her sister,
when they sprang the roadblock.

They didn't want her papers,
just held her back while the chopper
landed on the road and unwound.
The Border Patrol team stumped
up the mesquite roadbank

dragging a bodybag, humped it
into the chopper, then looked
away while it dispersed skyward.

She was then free to go.

Ay! How her heart
was heavy, then.
Twenty years after
she crossed the same desert,

what dangers she knew.
And the stories
her grandmother once told
of the uncle she never met

who left one day for *El Norte*
laden with promises,
stepping out under a bright sky
and that was all.

At least, tonight
they found a body.

TECTONIC

Disturbed plates of raw humanity
                sliding across the globe,
          quicksilver overlays
     on the crusted earth's faultlines.
           There's no known seismographs
               to gauge these eruptions.

We know, of course,
        that somewhere
        ethnic grievances throb

              that droughts spread out
                  across the lands,
                       while economies
      are pumped up or plundered down, but then
Surprise!
       A war breaks out,
           or ethnic cleansing, or blockades, or random chaos,
       spills over
          rumbles down hillsides,
    blood blooms through river deltas:
          executions, rapings, fire from the sky.

And people begin to shift, expelled by forces
                  as calculated as the Richter Scale,
       they drift
         because they know their children are hungry
              and will
           be chewed up by machines.

Bits of families, strangers holding hands,

they come,
    with unanticipated speed,
        in waves
on leaky rafts, on boxcars, or blistered feet
on their last
                drips of adrenaline.

O puny border walls
    did you believe you'd hold against
        the white-hot lava of their pain?

    These few who escape
                    at least for a time,
        will lie down and breathe
for a night   a beautiful shining night
                    worn and disbelieving
    until the next   upheaval.

WHAT THE UNCLES SAY

Ay, Chema,
those *coyotes*, they promised you
this wouldn't be so hard, didn't they?
Just a day's walk
from the border to the highway
and then the van to carry you on to Phoenix.
They took all your money,
said, come quickly now,
follow us. Chema, we all know
what happens after that:
On your second day of walking
a helicopter drops from the sky,
buzzes your group,
and in the blinding dust and noise,
those green-clad men on ATVs
zoom in, they scatter you
and hunt down stragglers.
You flatten, lizard-like
behind some boulders
and wait for dark, all alone.
Then it's day again, and canyons walls
curve and twist like red rock curtains
hiding the distant mountains
they said you should aim for.
This sun, it just hangs all over you,
refuses to blink or give direction.
Chema, what will become of you,
wandering and wandering, and this thirst
that tries to pull your throat apart?

Maybe you will find a cattle trough
thick with scum, and you will drink
then vomit all that is left in you.
Perhaps you will come across a cache
left by Samaritans: a jug of pure water,
a can of beans to sustain you moving on.
Perhaps a militiaman slashed the jug,
its brittle gallon shell mocks you in the dust.
Or there will be nothing to find, nothing at all,
and your weakened circles will wind down.
Or else another patrol will grab you anyway,
zip-tie you up, fling you like roadkill
back over the border,
broke and thirsty
to start over.

LOGBOOK (1)

Waypoint #3461

Found: 10 gallons water, 7 cans of beans

Left: none

Note: No activity at this site in over a month.

RELOCATION

After breakfast, someone spotted a rattlesnake sunning between the clinic tent and the kitchen, maybe two and a half feet long. We gave it a wide berth but the four Honduran patients who came in last night got all excited, grabbed sticks and a shovel, herded the snake into a drywall bucket and slammed a lid on. Big discussion ensued about what to do with the snake. E. said most desert reptiles will die if moved more than a mile from their familiar habitat. Further discussion weighing our livelihoods against that of the snake. Finally, a consensus to transport the bucketed snake to a comfortable gully about a mile north of camp. E. volunteered to drive, I got up on the truck bed with the bucket. I kept the lid clamped under my thighs as we bumped along a dry wash, trying not to listen to the indignant rattles of my captive passenger. About a half-mile out of camp, a Border Patrol chopper popped up over a ridge and buzzed us close, twice, scanning for migrants. E. kept on driving and I rehearsed what I would say if they landed and asked to see what we were carrying in the bucket. But they pulled away and we arrived safely at the gully. A quick lid-pry, and I gingerly pitched the disgruntled snake over the edge into his new environs.

MOUNTAIN

Tohono O'odham people
consider the mountain Navel of the Universe
swelling up through the world's belly.

Here the earth opened, and first peoples
emerged after the flood,
they called it Baboquivari.

It rises, purple-streaked
to where Earth meets Sky,
where People-world meets Spirit-world.

They say you should not go there without goodness in your
heart.

Elder Brother, I'itoi, watches over
all things from the high places there.
His home is a cave among cliffs.

They say if you are good, and bring gifts for I'itoi
the cave may make itself known.
If you are large, it will widen

so you can fit through. If you are small,
it will shrink so you may climb down inside.
You will be in the center of all things.

The tired, thirsty people
who now are streaming from the South,
they are told the shape of Baboquivari.

They are taught to keep it to their left
while walking, so they may reach
their new homes in the North.
Once a man, a rancher, claimed
he owned the lands surrounding
Baboquivari. Imagine! Owned the lands!

The story is he somehow found his way
into I'itoi's cave, and he broke
dishes, and stole some beads.

That night, flames rose up the flanks
of Baboquivari all around, and everything
that could be grazed was consumed.

LOGBOOK (2)

Waypoint #5145

Found: 4 gallons water half-emptied and full
of wasps, 2 old blankets, 1 bucket used as a latrine.

Left: 6 gallons water, 1 case of beans, 1 clean
bucket of granola bars/Vienna sausages.

Note: site was 200 yards further up the wash than
expected, hard to find.

hhooOOOOUUAAAAAGHHhhhhh

we feel them before we hear them before we see them before
we would be able to find cover if they were on a hostile
mission: two A-10 Warthog ground attack jets holding tight
formation each set of flaming twin turbofans throttled out full
roar low-altitude ground contour-hugging maneuvers out of
Davis-Monthan AFB Tucson bearing west-north-west towards
the Goldwater Bombing Range crossing over the Tohono
O'odham Nation is that an airspace violation while hanging
full ordinance racks on a routine training approach passing
just south of our camp third time this week the reverberations
linger through our bodies long after they are gone

A CAN OF PINTO BEANS

Just below the ridgeline saddle
tossed to the side of the trail
lying dented among rocks,
bleached label peeled back,
and the downhill-facing end
of the can stabbed through
by some Border Patrol agent's
Ka-Bar knife, a precise wound
mouldering around the edges,
with filaments wafting down
the corners, no, they're streams
of tiny ants, crawling in and out,
bearing flecks of nourishment away.

MOO

There is a tower on the edge of town,
bolted to the concrete pad they poured,
bone-white columns craning for a panoramic view
into citizens' backyards, into the labyrinth of arroyos
where migrants sometimes scattered through at dusk.
They studded the scaffolding with vigilant devices:
microphones, motion detectors, infrared cameras
all set to summon Border Patrol squads when tripped.
They called it "Virtual Fence," and gave Boeing
a generous billion for a pilot project, planting a string
of towers across the Arivaca sector. But the devices
were triggered by dust storms, rain showers, even
passing cattle, sending BP agents on frenzied roundups
ending in a moo. So they shut the system down,
left the structures dormant. And cows now
graze the mesquite groves in peace.

"Canyon Drop" site

> Found: numerous empty gallons and bean cans, garbage
>
> Left: 17 gallons water, 3 cases beans
>
> Note: 3 hour hike in to remote drop on well-used migrant trail. Lost keys to the truck, had to wait until nightfall for 2nd team to pick us up; evacuation closely monitored by Border Patrol agents in 2 vehicles, who followed us all the way into Nogales.
>
> Drop site remains secure.

DUSK

Dayheat leaves the earth
    all of a moment

Ay! how the known world rotates,
    mesquite shadows
        layering a bleached desert floor

Mourning doves take up
    their mourning

    First stars

Down-canyon, migrants emerge
        from crevasses
    bearing water jugs markered
    with the Sacred Heart
      and *¡Vaya con Dios!*

They point their feet
across a blinkered threshold

    as darkness

        scrubs
          the rockfaces

HELLO KITTY BACKPACK

— Ajo, Arizona

I came upon you
twelve miles from the nearest paved road.

Prim magenta bow above one ear
unblinking face
tipped up into the sun
from your peppermint pink zippered pocket.

Kitty, surely you must know
all things in the desert fade and crack
but you seem serene
one paw raised, a demure shrug.

It's one-hundred-and-ten degrees today
hushed but for the pulse in my ears
the clink of a kicked rock.

You are so petite.

A change of clothes, a liter water bottle
would overwhelm your empty belly.

Kitty, I don't want to know
the story of this destination
and as for your travel

companion,

SCAPULA

One afternoon, returning from a remote water cache, we spotted a scapula, a human shoulder blade, angling up from the sunbaked hardpan, stark white and triangular like a distant sail, motionless in the heat. No other bones lay about, so it must have been scavenged by an animal and dragged from the corpse, from one of the thousands of untended final resting places of bodies who have disappeared while crossing through the borderlands. We left the scapula undisturbed, filing by in a brief, inadequate moment of reverence. We marked the location as precisely as we could, so the county coroner might one day retrieve the bone, with the audacious hope that they could link it to a known missing person, give someone's survivors a shred, a closure. Someone whose life was carved out, leaving only this.

FIGURES

Ancient cave, cup of shade
a scoop in the canyon wall

the entrance littered with flattened
cans of Red Bull, tattery t-shirts,

a limp knapsack
silvering in the sun.

You can feel the fatigue
of those who rested here,

one more toehold
on the claw toward *El Norte.*

If they raised their eyes to the ceiling
they might have seen

two ochre stick figures, hand-in-hand,
looking down on them—

how many centuries,
how many passers-by,

O'odham people bearing
squash and castor beans

from Sonoran highlands
south to the Gulf of California

returning with dried fish
in labyrinthine baskets,

succession of feet carving paths
up and down the Mesoamerican spine.

In the cool of the evening, this generation
will reshoulder their burdens

head past the sacred mountain on the left,
northward towards the bulge of Kitts Peak

bristling with crazy gringo devices
for watching and listening to the stars,

and somewhere up there
a ship named Voyager

inscribed with a man and a woman
and its path through the planets

slides further on
from home.

ACKNOWLEDGMENTS

Construction: Figures

Cutthroat: A Journal of the Arts: Human Remains

Halfway Down the Stairs: As Thomas

Kissing Dynamite: Water Bearer

Pangyrus: A Can of Pinto Beans

Passengers Journal: Tectonic

Naugatuck River Review: Memo to the Border Patrol Agent Who Dumped Out the Water We Had Left in the Desert

Pithead Chapel: Scapula

We Refugees: A Pact Press Anthology: Dusk; What the Uncles Say

NOTES

These poems and fragments arise from my experience of
volunteering with an extraordinary organization called No
More Deaths / No Mas Muertes, which provides medical care
and material support for migrants passing through remote
and rugged sections of the Sonoran Desert along the Arizona-
Mexico border, and monitors for human rights abuses by bor-
der security forces. Over several years prior to the COVID-19
pandemic I spent a week or two each summer carrying water,
food and blankets out to remote locations along paths traveled
by migrants, and providing first aid and basic health care to
people who came through the desert base camp outside of
Arivaca, Arizona. I have a deep gratitude for the commitment
of the No More Deaths coordinators, and all the work they
do to save lives and seek justice for people on a desperate,
dangerous journey.

Territory Acknowledgment: the incidents described in these
pages mostly take place on Tohono O'odham lands. The To-
hono O'odham Nation is bisected by the border wall separat-
ing the colonial settler nations of the United States of America
and Mexico, and Tohono O'odham people endure frequent
overflights and incursions into their sovereign land by military
and security forces.

I dedicate this book to the thousands of people, known and
unknown, who have died on the journey through these bor-
derlands while seeking a better life for themselves and their
families.

ABOUT THE AUTHOR

Robbie Gamble's poems have appeared in the *Atlanta Review,*
Cutthroat, Pacifica Literary Review, Poet Lore, RHINO, Rust +
Moth, Slipstream, and *Whale Road Review,* among other jour-
nals. Recipient of the *Carve* Poetry prize, and a Peter
Taylor Fellowship at the Kenyon Summer Writers Workshop,
he holds an MFA from Lesley University, and he serves as
poetry editor for *Solstice: A Magazine of Diverse Voices.* Robbie
worked for twenty years as a nurse practitioner with Boston
Health Care for the Homeless Program, and he now divides
his time between Boston and Vermont.